MINDFULNESS JOURNAL FOR TEENS
DAILY CHECK-IN

MINDFULNESS JOURNAL FOR TEENS
DAILY CHECK-IN

Prompts to Help You Record and Grow Your Mindfulness Practice

KRISTEN MANIERI

ROCKRIDGE
PRESS

Interior and Cover Designer: Diana Haas
Art Producer: Janice Ackerman
Production Editor: Andrew Yackira
Production Manager: Michael Kay

Author photo courtesy of Arlene Laboy

ISBN: Print 978-1-63807-813-5
R0

THIS BOOK BELONGS TO:

_____

INTRODUCTION

You have an inner guidance system available to you when you pause and turn inward. This journal has been designed to be the space for that self-reflection, inviting you to engage with your wonderful work in progress: this life project called "you."

If it feels like you're in a constant state of flux, that's because you are. In the years between childhood and adulthood, your mind goes through a tremendous transformation. It can feel justifiably overwhelming as you seek to understand yourself, the world around you, and your place in it.

While it may feel turbulent, with its high-highs and low-lows, there is a way to feel more grounded: through practicing mindfulness.

Mindfulness—your ability to bring a curious and judgment-free awareness to the experiences inside and around you— gives you access to your inner captain. When you're present to your thoughts and emotions, you're not only able to witness yourself, but you're learning to direct and re-regulate yourself. You start to see that you can steer yourself in any direction you wish to go. It just takes practice. Pausing to take three deep breaths, scanning your body for tension and anxiety, and taking a moment to simply check in with yourself are all ways you can practice moving more gracefully (and quickly) through uncertain times.

As you meet yourself on the following pages for the next 90 days, you'll get to know yourself better and tap into your limitless capacity to grow, change, and evolve. Let's get started.

What's on my mind today?

_____

_____

_____

What deserves my energy and focus today?

_____

_____

What would being good to myself look like today?

_____

Ways I intend to feel grounded today:

○ THREE DEEP BREATHS

○ 60-SECOND BODY SCAN

○ MINDFUL CHECK-IN

I have the power to change:

_____

_____

_____

MY WORD OF THE DAY IS: _____

EVENING REFLECTIONS

What one thing can I be grateful for in this moment?

_____

I'm willing to let go of:

_____

Use this space to track how you practiced mindfulness throughout the day.

	WHEN	WHERE
MORNING		
AFTERNOON		
EVENING		

TODAY'S BEST MOMENTS:

What's on my mind today?

_____

_____

_____

What deserves my energy and focus today?

_____

_____

What would being good to myself look like today?

_____

Ways I intend to feel grounded today:

○ THREE DEEP BREATHS

○ 60-SECOND BODY SCAN

○ MINDFUL CHECK-IN

I have the power to change:

_____

_____

_____

MY WORD OF THE DAY IS: _____

EVENING REFLECTIONS

What one thing can I be grateful for in this moment?

_____

I'm willing to let go of:

_____

Use this space to track how you practiced mindfulness throughout the day.

	WHEN	WHERE
MORNING		
AFTERNOON		
EVENING		

TODAY'S BEST MOMENTS:

MORNING INTENTIONS

What's on my mind today?

_____

_____

_____

What deserves my energy and focus today?

_____

_____

What would being good to myself look like today?

_____

Ways I intend to feel grounded today:

○ THREE DEEP BREATHS

○ 60-SECOND BODY SCAN

○ MINDFUL CHECK-IN

I have the power to change:

_____

_____

_____

MY WORD OF THE DAY IS: _____

What one thing can I be grateful for in this moment?

_____

I'm willing to let go of:

_____

Use this space to track how you practiced mindfulness throughout the day.

	WHEN	WHERE
MORNING		
AFTERNOON		
EVENING		

TODAY'S BEST MOMENTS:

What's on my mind today?

_____

_____

_____

What deserves my energy and focus today?

_____

_____

What would being good to myself look like today?

_____

Ways I intend to feel grounded today:

○ THREE DEEP BREATHS

○ 60-SECOND BODY SCAN

○ MINDFUL CHECK-IN

I have the power to change:

_____

_____

_____

MY WORD OF THE DAY IS: _____

EVENING REFLECTIONS

What one thing can I be grateful for in this moment?

_____

I'm willing to let go of:

_____

Use this space to track how you practiced mindfulness throughout the day.

	WHEN	WHERE
MORNING		
AFTERNOON		
EVENING		

TODAY'S BEST MOMENTS:

MORNING INTENTIONS

What's on my mind today?

_____

_____

_____

What deserves my energy and focus today?

_____

_____

What would being good to myself look like today?

_____

Ways I intend to feel grounded today:

○ THREE DEEP BREATHS

○ 60-SECOND BODY SCAN

○ MINDFUL CHECK-IN

I have the power to change:

_____

_____

_____

MY WORD OF THE DAY IS: _____

EVENING REFLECTIONS

What one thing can I be grateful for in this moment?

_____

I'm willing to let go of:

_____

Use this space to track how you practiced mindfulness throughout the day.

	WHEN	WHERE
MORNING		
AFTERNOON		
EVENING		

TODAY'S BEST MOMENTS:

MORNING INTENTIONS

What's on my mind today?

_____

_____

_____

What deserves my energy and focus today?

_____

_____

What would being good to myself look like today?

_____

Ways I intend to feel grounded today:

○ THREE DEEP BREATHS

○ 60-SECOND BODY SCAN

○ MINDFUL CHECK-IN

I have the power to change:

_____

_____

_____

MY WORD OF THE DAY IS: _____

EVENING REFLECTIONS

What one thing can I be grateful for in this moment?

_____

I'm willing to let go of:

_____

Use this space to track how you practiced mindfulness throughout the day.

	WHEN	WHERE
MORNING		
AFTERNOON		
EVENING		

TODAY'S BEST MOMENTS:

MORNING INTENTIONS

What's on my mind today?

_____

_____

_____

What deserves my energy and focus today?

_____

_____

What would being good to myself look like today?

_____

Ways I intend to feel grounded today:

○ THREE DEEP BREATHS

○ 60-SECOND BODY SCAN

○ MINDFUL CHECK-IN

I have the power to change:

_____

_____

_____

MY WORD OF THE DAY IS: _____

EVENING REFLECTIONS

What one thing can I be grateful for in this moment?

_____

I'm willing to let go of:

_____

Use this space to track how you practiced mindfulness throughout the day.

	WHEN	WHERE
MORNING		
AFTERNOON		
EVENING		

TODAY'S BEST MOMENTS:

MORNING INTENTIONS

What's on my mind today?

_____

_____

_____

What deserves my energy and focus today?

_____

_____

What would being good to myself look like today?

_____

Ways I intend to feel grounded today:

○ THREE DEEP BREATHS

○ 60-SECOND BODY SCAN

○ MINDFUL CHECK-IN

I have the power to change:

_____

_____

_____

MY WORD OF THE DAY IS: _____

EVENING REFLECTIONS

What one thing can I be grateful for in this moment?

_____

I'm willing to let go of:

_____

Use this space to track how you practiced mindfulness throughout the day.

	WHEN	WHERE
MORNING		
AFTERNOON		
EVENING		

TODAY'S BEST MOMENTS:

MORNING INTENTIONS

What's on my mind today?

_____

_____

_____

What deserves my energy and focus today?

_____

_____

What would being good to myself look like today?

_____

Ways I intend to feel grounded today:

○ THREE DEEP BREATHS

○ 60-SECOND BODY SCAN

○ MINDFUL CHECK-IN

I have the power to change:

_____

_____

_____

MY WORD OF THE DAY IS: _____

EVENING REFLECTIONS

What one thing can I be grateful for in this moment?

_____

I'm willing to let go of:

_____

Use this space to track how you practiced mindfulness throughout the day.

	WHEN	WHERE
MORNING		
AFTERNOON		
EVENING		

TODAY'S BEST MOMENTS:

MORNING INTENTIONS

DATE: ___ / ___ / ___

What's on my mind today?

_____

_____

_____

What deserves my energy and focus today?

_____

_____

What would being good to myself look like today?

_____

Ways I intend to feel grounded today:

○ THREE DEEP BREATHS

○ 60-SECOND BODY SCAN

○ MINDFUL CHECK-IN

I have the power to change:

_____

_____

_____

MY WORD OF THE DAY IS: _____

20   Mindfulness Journal for Teens

EVENING REFLECTIONS

What one thing can I be grateful for in this moment?

_____

I'm willing to let go of:

_____

Use this space to track how you practiced mindfulness throughout the day.

	WHEN	WHERE
MORNING		
AFTERNOON		
EVENING		

TODAY'S BEST MOMENTS:

MORNING INTENTIONS

What's on my mind today?

_____

_____

_____

What deserves my energy and focus today?

_____

_____

What would being good to myself look like today?

_____

Ways I intend to feel grounded today:

○ THREE DEEP BREATHS

○ 60-SECOND BODY SCAN

○ MINDFUL CHECK-IN

I have the power to change:

_____

_____

_____

MY WORD OF THE DAY IS: _____

EVENING REFLECTIONS

What one thing can I be grateful for in this moment?

_____

I'm willing to let go of:

_____

Use this space to track how you practiced mindfulness throughout the day.

	WHEN	WHERE
MORNING		
AFTERNOON		
EVENING		

TODAY'S BEST MOMENTS:

DATE: ___ / ___ / ___

What's on my mind today?

_____

_____

_____

What deserves my energy and focus today?

_____

_____

What would being good to myself look like today?

_____

Ways I intend to feel grounded today:

○ THREE DEEP BREATHS

○ 60-SECOND BODY SCAN

○ MINDFUL CHECK-IN

I have the power to change:

_____

_____

_____

MY WORD OF THE DAY IS: _____

EVENING REFLECTIONS

What one thing can I be grateful for in this moment?

_____

I'm willing to let go of:

_____

Use this space to track how you practiced mindfulness throughout the day.

	WHEN	WHERE
MORNING		
AFTERNOON		
EVENING		

TODAY'S BEST MOMENTS:

MORNING INTENTIONS

DATE: ___ / ___ / ___

What's on my mind today?

_____

_____

_____

What deserves my energy and focus today?

_____

_____

What would being good to myself look like today?

_____

Ways I intend to feel grounded today:

○ THREE DEEP BREATHS

○ 60-SECOND BODY SCAN

○ MINDFUL CHECK-IN

I have the power to change:

_____

_____

_____

MY WORD OF THE DAY IS: _____

EVENING REFLECTIONS

What one thing can I be grateful for in this moment?

_____

I'm willing to let go of:

_____

Use this space to track how you practiced mindfulness throughout the day.

	WHEN	WHERE
MORNING		
AFTERNOON		
EVENING		

TODAY'S BEST MOMENTS:

MORNING INTENTIONS

What's on my mind today?

_____

_____

_____

What deserves my energy and focus today?

_____

_____

What would being good to myself look like today?

_____

Ways I intend to feel grounded today:

○ THREE DEEP BREATHS

○ 60-SECOND BODY SCAN

○ MINDFUL CHECK-IN

I have the power to change:

_____

_____

_____

MY WORD OF THE DAY IS: _____

EVENING REFLECTIONS

What one thing can I be grateful for in this moment?

_____

I'm willing to let go of:

_____

Use this space to track how you practiced mindfulness throughout the day.

	WHEN	WHERE
MORNING		
AFTERNOON		
EVENING		

TODAY'S BEST MOMENTS:

What's on my mind today?

_____

_____

_____

What deserves my energy and focus today?

_____

_____

What would being good to myself look like today?

_____

Ways I intend to feel grounded today:

○ THREE DEEP BREATHS

○ 60-SECOND BODY SCAN

○ MINDFUL CHECK-IN

I have the power to change:

_____

_____

_____

MY WORD OF THE DAY IS: _____

EVENING REFLECTIONS

What one thing can I be grateful for in this moment?

_____

I'm willing to let go of:

_____

Use this space to track how you practiced mindfulness throughout the day.

	WHEN	WHERE
MORNING		
AFTERNOON		
EVENING		

TODAY'S BEST MOMENTS:

MORNING INTENTIONS

What's on my mind today?

_____

_____

_____

What deserves my energy and focus today?

_____

_____

What would being good to myself look like today?

_____

Ways I intend to feel grounded today:

○ THREE DEEP BREATHS

○ 60-SECOND BODY SCAN

○ MINDFUL CHECK-IN

I have the power to change:

_____

_____

_____

MY WORD OF THE DAY IS: _____

EVENING REFLECTIONS

What one thing can I be grateful for in this moment?

_____

I'm willing to let go of:

_____

Use this space to track how you practiced mindfulness throughout the day.

	WHEN	WHERE
MORNING		
AFTERNOON		
EVENING		

TODAY'S BEST MOMENTS:

MORNING INTENTIONS

What's on my mind today?

_____

_____

_____

What deserves my energy and focus today?

_____

_____

What would being good to myself look like today?

_____

Ways I intend to feel grounded today:

○ THREE DEEP BREATHS

○ 60-SECOND BODY SCAN

○ MINDFUL CHECK-IN

I have the power to change:

_____

_____

_____

MY WORD OF THE DAY IS: _____

EVENING REFLECTIONS

What one thing can I be grateful for in this moment?

_____

I'm willing to let go of:

_____

Use this space to track how you practiced mindfulness throughout the day.

	WHEN	WHERE
MORNING		
AFTERNOON		
EVENING		

TODAY'S BEST MOMENTS:

MORNING INTENTIONS

What's on my mind today?

_____

_____

_____

What deserves my energy and focus today?

_____

_____

What would being good to myself look like today?

_____

Ways I intend to feel grounded today:

○ THREE DEEP BREATHS

○ 60-SECOND BODY SCAN

○ MINDFUL CHECK-IN

I have the power to change:

_____

_____

_____

MY WORD OF THE DAY IS: _____

EVENING REFLECTIONS

What one thing can I be grateful for in this moment?

_____

I'm willing to let go of:

_____

Use this space to track how you practiced mindfulness throughout the day.

	WHEN	WHERE
MORNING		
AFTERNOON		
EVENING		

TODAY'S BEST MOMENTS:

MORNING INTENTIONS

What's on my mind today?

_____

_____

_____

What deserves my energy and focus today?

_____

_____

What would being good to myself look like today?

_____

Ways I intend to feel grounded today:

○ THREE DEEP BREATHS

○ 60-SECOND BODY SCAN

○ MINDFUL CHECK-IN

I have the power to change:

_____

_____

_____

MY WORD OF THE DAY IS: _____

EVENING REFLECTIONS

What one thing can I be grateful for in this moment?

_____

I'm willing to let go of:

_____

Use this space to track how you practiced mindfulness throughout the day.

	WHEN	WHERE
MORNING		
AFTERNOON		
EVENING		

TODAY'S BEST MOMENTS:

MORNING INTENTIONS

What's on my mind today?

_____

_____

_____

What deserves my energy and focus today?

_____

_____

What would being good to myself look like today?

_____

Ways I intend to feel grounded today:

○ THREE DEEP BREATHS

○ 60-SECOND BODY SCAN

○ MINDFUL CHECK-IN

I have the power to change:

_____

_____

_____

MY WORD OF THE DAY IS: _____

What one thing can I be grateful for in this moment?

_____

I'm willing to let go of:

_____

Use this space to track how you practiced mindfulness throughout the day.

	WHEN	WHERE
MORNING		
AFTERNOON		
EVENING		

TODAY'S BEST MOMENTS:

DATE: ___ / ___ / ___

What's on my mind today?

_____

_____

_____

What deserves my energy and focus today?

_____

_____

What would being good to myself look like today?

_____

Ways I intend to feel grounded today:

○ THREE DEEP BREATHS

○ 60-SECOND BODY SCAN

○ MINDFUL CHECK-IN

I have the power to change:

_____

_____

_____

MY WORD OF THE DAY IS: _____

EVENING REFLECTIONS

What one thing can I be grateful for in this moment?

_____

I'm willing to let go of:

_____

Use this space to track how you practiced mindfulness throughout the day.

	WHEN	WHERE
MORNING		
AFTERNOON		
EVENING		

TODAY'S BEST MOMENTS:

MORNING INTENTIONS

What's on my mind today?

_____

_____

_____

What deserves my energy and focus today?

_____

_____

What would being good to myself look like today?

_____

Ways I intend to feel grounded today:

○ THREE DEEP BREATHS

○ 60-SECOND BODY SCAN

○ MINDFUL CHECK-IN

I have the power to change:

_____

_____

_____

MY WORD OF THE DAY IS: _____

EVENING REFLECTIONS

What one thing can I be grateful for in this moment?

_____

I'm willing to let go of:

_____

Use this space to track how you practiced mindfulness throughout the day.

	WHEN	WHERE
MORNING		
AFTERNOON		
EVENING		

TODAY'S BEST MOMENTS:

DATE: ___ / ___ / ___

What's on my mind today?

_____

_____

_____

What deserves my energy and focus today?

_____

_____

What would being good to myself look like today?

_____

Ways I intend to feel grounded today:

◯ THREE DEEP BREATHS

◯ 60-SECOND BODY SCAN

◯ MINDFUL CHECK-IN

I have the power to change:

_____

_____

_____

MY WORD OF THE DAY IS: _____

EVENING REFLECTIONS

What one thing can I be grateful for in this moment?

_____

I'm willing to let go of:

_____

Use this space to track how you practiced mindfulness throughout the day.

	WHEN	WHERE
MORNING		
AFTERNOON		
EVENING		

TODAY'S BEST MOMENTS:

MORNING INTENTIONS

What's on my mind today?

_____

_____

_____

What deserves my energy and focus today?

_____

_____

What would being good to myself look like today?

_____

Ways I intend to feel grounded today:

○ THREE DEEP BREATHS

○ 60-SECOND BODY SCAN

○ MINDFUL CHECK-IN

I have the power to change:

_____

_____

_____

MY WORD OF THE DAY IS: _____

EVENING REFLECTIONS

What one thing can I be grateful for in this moment?

_____

I'm willing to let go of:

_____

Use this space to track how you practiced mindfulness throughout the day.

	WHEN	WHERE
MORNING		
AFTERNOON		
EVENING		

TODAY'S BEST MOMENTS:

MORNING INTENTIONS

What's on my mind today?

_____

_____

_____

What deserves my energy and focus today?

_____

_____

What would being good to myself look like today?

_____

Ways I intend to feel grounded today:

○ THREE DEEP BREATHS

○ 60-SECOND BODY SCAN

○ MINDFUL CHECK-IN

I have the power to change:

_____

_____

_____

MY WORD OF THE DAY IS: _____

EVENING REFLECTIONS

What one thing can I be grateful for in this moment?

_____

I'm willing to let go of:

_____

Use this space to track how you practiced mindfulness throughout the day.

	WHEN	WHERE
MORNING		
AFTERNOON		
EVENING		

TODAY'S BEST MOMENTS:

MORNING INTENTIONS

What's on my mind today?

_____

_____

_____

What deserves my energy and focus today?

_____

_____

What would being good to myself look like today?

_____

Ways I intend to feel grounded today:

○ THREE DEEP BREATHS

○ 60-SECOND BODY SCAN

○ MINDFUL CHECK-IN

I have the power to change:

_____

_____

_____

MY WORD OF THE DAY IS: _____

EVENING REFLECTIONS

What one thing can I be grateful for in this moment?

_____

I'm willing to let go of:

_____

Use this space to track how you practiced mindfulness throughout the day.

	WHEN	WHERE
MORNING		
AFTERNOON		
EVENING		

TODAY'S BEST MOMENTS:

MORNING INTENTIONS

What's on my mind today?

_____

_____

_____

What deserves my energy and focus today?

_____

_____

What would being good to myself look like today?

_____

Ways I intend to feel grounded today:

○ THREE DEEP BREATHS

○ 60-SECOND BODY SCAN

○ MINDFUL CHECK-IN

I have the power to change:

_____

_____

_____

MY WORD OF THE DAY IS: _____

EVENING REFLECTIONS

What one thing can I be grateful for in this moment?

_____

I'm willing to let go of:

_____

Use this space to track how you practiced mindfulness throughout the day.

	WHEN	WHERE
MORNING		
AFTERNOON		
EVENING		

TODAY'S BEST MOMENTS:

MORNING INTENTIONS

What's on my mind today?

_____

_____

_____

What deserves my energy and focus today?

_____

_____

What would being good to myself look like today?

_____

Ways I intend to feel grounded today:

○ THREE DEEP BREATHS

○ 60-SECOND BODY SCAN

○ MINDFUL CHECK-IN

I have the power to change:

_____

_____

_____

MY WORD OF THE DAY IS: _____

EVENING REFLECTIONS

What one thing can I be grateful for in this moment?

_____

I'm willing to let go of:

_____

Use this space to track how you practiced mindfulness throughout the day.

	WHEN	WHERE
MORNING		
AFTERNOON		
EVENING		

TODAY'S BEST MOMENTS:

What's on my mind today?

_____

_____

_____

What deserves my energy and focus today?

_____

_____

What would being good to myself look like today?

_____

Ways I intend to feel grounded today:

○ THREE DEEP BREATHS

○ 60-SECOND BODY SCAN

○ MINDFUL CHECK-IN

I have the power to change:

_____

_____

_____

MY WORD OF THE DAY IS: _____

EVENING REFLECTIONS

What one thing can I be grateful for in this moment?

_____

I'm willing to let go of:

_____

Use this space to track how you practiced mindfulness throughout the day.

	WHEN	WHERE
MORNING		
AFTERNOON		
EVENING		

TODAY'S BEST MOMENTS:

MORNING INTENTIONS

What's on my mind today?

_____

_____

_____

What deserves my energy and focus today?

_____

_____

What would being good to myself look like today?

_____

Ways I intend to feel grounded today:

○ THREE DEEP BREATHS

○ 60-SECOND BODY SCAN

○ MINDFUL CHECK-IN

I have the power to change:

_____

_____

_____

MY WORD OF THE DAY IS: _____

EVENING REFLECTIONS

What one thing can I be grateful for in this moment?

_____

I'm willing to let go of:

_____

Use this space to track how you practiced mindfulness throughout the day.

	WHEN	WHERE
MORNING		
AFTERNOON		
EVENING		

TODAY'S BEST MOMENTS:

DATE: ___ / ___ / ___

What's on my mind today?

_____

_____

_____

What deserves my energy and focus today?

_____

_____

What would being good to myself look like today?

_____

Ways I intend to feel grounded today:

○ THREE DEEP BREATHS

○ 60-SECOND BODY SCAN

○ MINDFUL CHECK-IN

I have the power to change:

_____

_____

_____

MY WORD OF THE DAY IS: _____

EVENING REFLECTIONS

What one thing can I be grateful for in this moment?

_____

I'm willing to let go of:

_____

Use this space to track how you practiced mindfulness throughout the day.

	WHEN	WHERE
MORNING		
AFTERNOON		
EVENING		

TODAY'S BEST MOMENTS:

MORNING INTENTIONS

What's on my mind today?

_____

_____

_____

What deserves my energy and focus today?

_____

_____

What would being good to myself look like today?

_____

Ways I intend to feel grounded today:

○ THREE DEEP BREATHS

○ 60-SECOND BODY SCAN

○ MINDFUL CHECK-IN

I have the power to change:

_____

_____

_____

MY WORD OF THE DAY IS: _____

EVENING REFLECTIONS

What one thing can I be grateful for in this moment?

_____

I'm willing to let go of:

_____

Use this space to track how you practiced mindfulness throughout the day.

	WHEN	WHERE
MORNING		
AFTERNOON		
EVENING		

TODAY'S BEST MOMENTS:

MORNING INTENTIONS

What's on my mind today?

_____

_____

_____

What deserves my energy and focus today?

_____

_____

What would being good to myself look like today?

_____

Ways I intend to feel grounded today:

○ THREE DEEP BREATHS

○ 60-SECOND BODY SCAN

○ MINDFUL CHECK-IN

I have the power to change:

_____

_____

_____

MY WORD OF THE DAY IS: _____

EVENING REFLECTIONS

What one thing can I be grateful for in this moment?

_____

I'm willing to let go of:

_____

Use this space to track how you practiced mindfulness throughout the day.

	WHEN	WHERE
MORNING		
AFTERNOON		
EVENING		

TODAY'S BEST MOMENTS:

MORNING INTENTIONS

What's on my mind today?

_____

_____

_____

What deserves my energy and focus today?

_____

_____

What would being good to myself look like today?

_____

Ways I intend to feel grounded today:

○ THREE DEEP BREATHS

○ 60-SECOND BODY SCAN

○ MINDFUL CHECK-IN

I have the power to change:

_____

_____

_____

MY WORD OF THE DAY IS: _____

EVENING REFLECTIONS

What one thing can I be grateful for in this moment?

_____

I'm willing to let go of:

_____

Use this space to track how you practiced mindfulness throughout the day.

	WHEN	WHERE
MORNING		
AFTERNOON		
EVENING		

TODAY'S BEST MOMENTS:

MORNING INTENTIONS

What's on my mind today?

_____

_____

_____

What deserves my energy and focus today?

_____

_____

What would being good to myself look like today?

_____

Ways I intend to feel grounded today:

○ THREE DEEP BREATHS

○ 60-SECOND BODY SCAN

○ MINDFUL CHECK-IN

I have the power to change:

_____

_____

_____

MY WORD OF THE DAY IS: _____

EVENING REFLECTIONS

What one thing can I be grateful for in this moment?

_____

I'm willing to let go of:

_____

Use this space to track how you practiced mindfulness throughout the day.

	WHEN	WHERE
MORNING		
AFTERNOON		
EVENING		

TODAY'S BEST MOMENTS:

What's on my mind today?

_____

_____

_____

What deserves my energy and focus today?

_____

_____

What would being good to myself look like today?

_____

Ways I intend to feel grounded today:

○ THREE DEEP BREATHS

○ 60-SECOND BODY SCAN

○ MINDFUL CHECK-IN

I have the power to change:

_____

_____

_____

MY WORD OF THE DAY IS: _____

EVENING REFLECTIONS

What one thing can I be grateful for in this moment?

_____

I'm willing to let go of:

_____

Use this space to track how you practiced mindfulness throughout the day.

	WHEN	WHERE
MORNING		
AFTERNOON		
EVENING		

TODAY'S BEST MOMENTS:

MORNING INTENTIONS

What's on my mind today?

_____

_____

_____

What deserves my energy and focus today?

_____

_____

What would being good to myself look like today?

_____

Ways I intend to feel grounded today:

○ THREE DEEP BREATHS

○ 60-SECOND BODY SCAN

○ MINDFUL CHECK-IN

I have the power to change:

_____

_____

_____

MY WORD OF THE DAY IS: _____

EVENING REFLECTIONS

What one thing can I be grateful for in this moment?

_____

I'm willing to let go of:

_____

Use this space to track how you practiced mindfulness throughout the day.

	WHEN	WHERE
MORNING		
AFTERNOON		
EVENING		

TODAY'S BEST MOMENTS:

MORNING INTENTIONS

What's on my mind today?

_____

_____

_____

What deserves my energy and focus today?

_____

_____

What would being good to myself look like today?

_____

Ways I intend to feel grounded today:

○ THREE DEEP BREATHS

○ 60-SECOND BODY SCAN

○ MINDFUL CHECK-IN

I have the power to change:

_____

_____

_____

MY WORD OF THE DAY IS: _____

EVENING REFLECTIONS

What one thing can I be grateful for in this moment?

_____

I'm willing to let go of:

_____

Use this space to track how you practiced mindfulness throughout the day.

	WHEN	WHERE
MORNING		
AFTERNOON		
EVENING		

TODAY'S BEST MOMENTS:

MORNING INTENTIONS

What's on my mind today?

_____

_____

_____

What deserves my energy and focus today?

_____

_____

What would being good to myself look like today?

_____

Ways I intend to feel grounded today:

○ THREE DEEP BREATHS

○ 60-SECOND BODY SCAN

○ MINDFUL CHECK-IN

I have the power to change:

_____

_____

_____

MY WORD OF THE DAY IS: _____

EVENING REFLECTIONS

What one thing can I be grateful for in this moment?

_____

I'm willing to let go of:

_____

Use this space to track how you practiced mindfulness throughout the day.

	WHEN	WHERE
MORNING		
AFTERNOON		
EVENING		

TODAY'S BEST MOMENTS:

MORNING INTENTIONS

What's on my mind today?

_____

_____

_____

What deserves my energy and focus today?

_____

_____

What would being good to myself look like today?

_____

Ways I intend to feel grounded today:

○ THREE DEEP BREATHS

○ 60-SECOND BODY SCAN

○ MINDFUL CHECK-IN

I have the power to change:

_____

_____

_____

MY WORD OF THE DAY IS: _____

EVENING REFLECTIONS

What one thing can I be grateful for in this moment?

_____

I'm willing to let go of:

_____

Use this space to track how you practiced mindfulness throughout the day.

	WHEN	WHERE
MORNING		
AFTERNOON		
EVENING		

TODAY'S BEST MOMENTS:

MORNING INTENTIONS

What's on my mind today?

_____

_____

_____

What deserves my energy and focus today?

_____

_____

What would being good to myself look like today?

_____

Ways I intend to feel grounded today:

○ THREE DEEP BREATHS

○ 60-SECOND BODY SCAN

○ MINDFUL CHECK-IN

I have the power to change:

_____

_____

_____

MY WORD OF THE DAY IS: _____

EVENING REFLECTIONS

What one thing can I be grateful for in this moment?

_____

I'm willing to let go of:

_____

Use this space to track how you practiced mindfulness throughout the day.

	WHEN	WHERE
MORNING		
AFTERNOON		
EVENING		

TODAY'S BEST MOMENTS:

MORNING INTENTIONS

What's on my mind today?

_____

_____

_____

What deserves my energy and focus today?

_____

_____

What would being good to myself look like today?

_____

Ways I intend to feel grounded today:

○ THREE DEEP BREATHS

○ 60-SECOND BODY SCAN

○ MINDFUL CHECK-IN

I have the power to change:

_____

_____

_____

MY WORD OF THE DAY IS: _____

EVENING REFLECTIONS

What one thing can I be grateful for in this moment?

_____

I'm willing to let go of:

_____

Use this space to track how you practiced mindfulness throughout the day.

	WHEN	WHERE
MORNING		
AFTERNOON		
EVENING		

TODAY'S BEST MOMENTS:

MORNING INTENTIONS

DATE: ___ / ___ / ___

What's on my mind today?

_____

_____

_____

What deserves my energy and focus today?

_____

_____

What would being good to myself look like today?

_____

Ways I intend to feel grounded today:

○ THREE DEEP BREATHS

○ 60-SECOND BODY SCAN

○ MINDFUL CHECK-IN

I have the power to change:

_____

_____

_____

MY WORD OF THE DAY IS: _____

EVENING REFLECTIONS

What one thing can I be grateful for in this moment?

_____

I'm willing to let go of:

_____

Use this space to track how you practiced mindfulness throughout the day.

	WHEN	WHERE
MORNING		
AFTERNOON		
EVENING		

TODAY'S BEST MOMENTS:

MORNING INTENTIONS

What's on my mind today?

_____

_____

_____

What deserves my energy and focus today?

_____

_____

What would being good to myself look like today?

_____

Ways I intend to feel grounded today:

○ THREE DEEP BREATHS

○ 60-SECOND BODY SCAN

○ MINDFUL CHECK-IN

I have the power to change:

_____

_____

_____

MY WORD OF THE DAY IS: _____

EVENING REFLECTIONS

What one thing can I be grateful for in this moment?

_____

I'm willing to let go of:

_____

Use this space to track how you practiced mindfulness throughout the day.

	WHEN	WHERE
MORNING		
AFTERNOON		
EVENING		

TODAY'S BEST MOMENTS:

MORNING INTENTIONS

What's on my mind today?

_____

_____

_____

What deserves my energy and focus today?

_____

_____

What would being good to myself look like today?

_____

Ways I intend to feel grounded today:

○ THREE DEEP BREATHS

○ 60-SECOND BODY SCAN

○ MINDFUL CHECK-IN

I have the power to change:

_____

_____

_____

MY WORD OF THE DAY IS: _____

EVENING REFLECTIONS

What one thing can I be grateful for in this moment?

_____

I'm willing to let go of:

_____

Use this space to track how you practiced mindfulness throughout the day.

	WHEN	WHERE
MORNING		
AFTERNOON		
EVENING		

TODAY'S BEST MOMENTS:

DATE: ___ / ___ / ___

What's on my mind today?

_____

_____

_____

What deserves my energy and focus today?

_____

_____

What would being good to myself look like today?

_____

Ways I intend to feel grounded today:

○ THREE DEEP BREATHS

○ 60-SECOND BODY SCAN

○ MINDFUL CHECK-IN

I have the power to change:

_____

_____

_____

MY WORD OF THE DAY IS: _____

EVENING REFLECTIONS

What one thing can I be grateful for in this moment?

_____

I'm willing to let go of:

_____

Use this space to track how you practiced mindfulness throughout the day.

	WHEN	WHERE
MORNING		
AFTERNOON		
EVENING		

TODAY'S BEST MOMENTS:

What's on my mind today?

_____

_____

_____

What deserves my energy and focus today?

_____

_____

What would being good to myself look like today?

_____

Ways I intend to feel grounded today:

○ THREE DEEP BREATHS

○ 60-SECOND BODY SCAN

○ MINDFUL CHECK-IN

I have the power to change:

_____

_____

_____

MY WORD OF THE DAY IS: _____

EVENING REFLECTIONS

What one thing can I be grateful for in this moment?

_____

I'm willing to let go of:

_____

Use this space to track how you practiced mindfulness throughout the day.

	WHEN	WHERE
MORNING		
AFTERNOON		
EVENING		

TODAY'S BEST MOMENTS:

MORNING INTENTIONS

What's on my mind today?

_____

_____

_____

What deserves my energy and focus today?

_____

_____

What would being good to myself look like today?

_____

Ways I intend to feel grounded today:

○ THREE DEEP BREATHS

○ 60-SECOND BODY SCAN

○ MINDFUL CHECK-IN

I have the power to change:

_____

_____

_____

MY WORD OF THE DAY IS: _____

DATE: ___ / ___ / ___   *EVENING REFLECTIONS*

What one thing can I be grateful for in this moment?

_____

I'm willing to let go of:

_____

Use this space to track how you practiced mindfulness
throughout the day.

	WHEN	WHERE
MORNING		
AFTERNOON		
EVENING		

TODAY'S BEST MOMENTS:

MORNING INTENTIONS

What's on my mind today?

_____

_____

_____

What deserves my energy and focus today?

_____

_____

What would being good to myself look like today?

_____

Ways I intend to feel grounded today:

○ THREE DEEP BREATHS

○ 60-SECOND BODY SCAN

○ MINDFUL CHECK-IN

I have the power to change:

_____

_____

_____

MY WORD OF THE DAY IS: _____

EVENING REFLECTIONS

What one thing can I be grateful for in this moment?

_____

I'm willing to let go of:

_____

Use this space to track how you practiced mindfulness throughout the day.

	WHEN	WHERE
MORNING		
AFTERNOON		
EVENING		

TODAY'S BEST MOMENTS:

MORNING INTENTIONS

DATE: ___ / ___ / ___

What's on my mind today?

_____

_____

_____

What deserves my energy and focus today?

_____

_____

What would being good to myself look like today?

_____

Ways I intend to feel grounded today:

○ THREE DEEP BREATHS

○ 60-SECOND BODY SCAN

○ MINDFUL CHECK-IN

I have the power to change:

_____

_____

_____

MY WORD OF THE DAY IS: _____

EVENING REFLECTIONS

What one thing can I be grateful for in this moment?

_____

I'm willing to let go of:

_____

Use this space to track how you practiced mindfulness throughout the day.

	WHEN	WHERE
MORNING		
AFTERNOON		
EVENING		

TODAY'S BEST MOMENTS:

MORNING INTENTIONS

What's on my mind today?

_____

_____

_____

What deserves my energy and focus today?

_____

_____

What would being good to myself look like today?

_____

Ways I intend to feel grounded today:

○ THREE DEEP BREATHS

○ 60-SECOND BODY SCAN

○ MINDFUL CHECK-IN

I have the power to change:

_____

_____

_____

MY WORD OF THE DAY IS: _____

EVENING REFLECTIONS

What one thing can I be grateful for in this moment?

_____

I'm willing to let go of:

_____

Use this space to track how you practiced mindfulness throughout the day.

	WHEN	WHERE
MORNING		
AFTERNOON		
EVENING		

TODAY'S BEST MOMENTS:

DATE: ___ / ___ / ___

What's on my mind today?

_____

_____

_____

What deserves my energy and focus today?

_____

_____

What would being good to myself look like today?

_____

Ways I intend to feel grounded today:

○ THREE DEEP BREATHS

○ 60-SECOND BODY SCAN

○ MINDFUL CHECK-IN

I have the power to change:

_____

_____

_____

MY WORD OF THE DAY IS: _____

EVENING REFLECTIONS

What one thing can I be grateful for in this moment?

_____

I'm willing to let go of:

_____

Use this space to track how you practiced mindfulness throughout the day.

	WHEN	WHERE
MORNING		
AFTERNOON		
EVENING		

TODAY'S BEST MOMENTS:

MORNING INTENTIONS

What's on my mind today?

_____

_____

_____

What deserves my energy and focus today?

_____

_____

What would being good to myself look like today?

_____

Ways I intend to feel grounded today:

○ THREE DEEP BREATHS

○ 60-SECOND BODY SCAN

○ MINDFUL CHECK-IN

I have the power to change:

_____

_____

_____

MY WORD OF THE DAY IS: _____

EVENING REFLECTIONS

What one thing can I be grateful for in this moment?

_____

I'm willing to let go of:

_____

Use this space to track how you practiced mindfulness throughout the day.

	WHEN	WHERE
MORNING		
AFTERNOON		
EVENING		

TODAY'S BEST MOMENTS:

MORNING INTENTIONS

What's on my mind today?

_____

_____

_____

What deserves my energy and focus today?

_____

_____

What would being good to myself look like today?

_____

Ways I intend to feel grounded today:

○ THREE DEEP BREATHS

○ 60-SECOND BODY SCAN

○ MINDFUL CHECK-IN

I have the power to change:

_____

_____

_____

MY WORD OF THE DAY IS: _____

EVENING REFLECTIONS

What one thing can I be grateful for in this moment?

_____

I'm willing to let go of:

_____

Use this space to track how you practiced mindfulness throughout the day.

	WHEN	WHERE
MORNING		
AFTERNOON		
EVENING		

TODAY'S BEST MOMENTS:

DATE: ___ / ___ / ___

What's on my mind today?

_____

_____

_____

What deserves my energy and focus today?

_____

_____

What would being good to myself look like today?

_____

Ways I intend to feel grounded today:

○ THREE DEEP BREATHS

○ 60-SECOND BODY SCAN

○ MINDFUL CHECK-IN

I have the power to change:

_____

_____

_____

MY WORD OF THE DAY IS: _____

EVENING REFLECTIONS

What one thing can I be grateful for in this moment?

_____

I'm willing to let go of:

_____

Use this space to track how you practiced mindfulness throughout the day.

	WHEN	WHERE
MORNING		
AFTERNOON		
EVENING		

TODAY'S BEST MOMENTS:

MORNING INTENTIONS

What's on my mind today?

_____

_____

_____

What deserves my energy and focus today?

_____

_____

What would being good to myself look like today?

_____

Ways I intend to feel grounded today:

○ THREE DEEP BREATHS

○ 60-SECOND BODY SCAN

○ MINDFUL CHECK-IN

I have the power to change:

_____

_____

_____

MY WORD OF THE DAY IS: _____

EVENING REFLECTIONS

What one thing can I be grateful for in this moment?

_____

I'm willing to let go of:

_____

Use this space to track how you practiced mindfulness throughout the day.

	WHEN	WHERE
MORNING		
AFTERNOON		
EVENING		

TODAY'S BEST MOMENTS:

MORNING INTENTIONS

What's on my mind today?

_____

_____

_____

What deserves my energy and focus today?

_____

_____

What would being good to myself look like today?

_____

Ways I intend to feel grounded today:

○ THREE DEEP BREATHS

○ 60-SECOND BODY SCAN

○ MINDFUL CHECK-IN

I have the power to change:

_____

_____

_____

MY WORD OF THE DAY IS: _____

EVENING REFLECTIONS

What one thing can I be grateful for in this moment?

_____

I'm willing to let go of:

_____

Use this space to track how you practiced mindfulness throughout the day.

	WHEN	WHERE
MORNING		
AFTERNOON		
EVENING		

TODAY'S BEST MOMENTS:

MORNING INTENTIONS

What's on my mind today?

_____

_____

_____

What deserves my energy and focus today?

_____

_____

What would being good to myself look like today?

_____

Ways I intend to feel grounded today:

○ THREE DEEP BREATHS

○ 60-SECOND BODY SCAN

○ MINDFUL CHECK-IN

I have the power to change:

_____

_____

_____

MY WORD OF THE DAY IS: _____

EVENING REFLECTIONS

What one thing can I be grateful for in this moment?

_____

I'm willing to let go of:

_____

Use this space to track how you practiced mindfulness throughout the day.

	WHEN	WHERE
MORNING		
AFTERNOON		
EVENING		

TODAY'S BEST MOMENTS:

MORNING INTENTIONS

What's on my mind today?

_____

_____

_____

What deserves my energy and focus today?

_____

_____

What would being good to myself look like today?

_____

Ways I intend to feel grounded today:

○ THREE DEEP BREATHS

○ 60-SECOND BODY SCAN

○ MINDFUL CHECK-IN

I have the power to change:

_____

_____

_____

MY WORD OF THE DAY IS: _____

EVENING REFLECTIONS

What one thing can I be grateful for in this moment?

_____

I'm willing to let go of:

_____

Use this space to track how you practiced mindfulness throughout the day.

	WHEN	WHERE
MORNING		
AFTERNOON		
EVENING		

TODAY'S BEST MOMENTS:

MORNING INTENTIONS

DATE: ___ / ___ / ___

What's on my mind today?

_____

_____

_____

What deserves my energy and focus today?

_____

_____

What would being good to myself look like today?

_____

Ways I intend to feel grounded today:

○ THREE DEEP BREATHS

○ 60-SECOND BODY SCAN

○ MINDFUL CHECK-IN

I have the power to change:

_____

_____

_____

MY WORD OF THE DAY IS: _____

EVENING REFLECTIONS

What one thing can I be grateful for in this moment?

_____

I'm willing to let go of:

_____

Use this space to track how you practiced mindfulness throughout the day.

	WHEN	WHERE
MORNING		
AFTERNOON		
EVENING		

TODAY'S BEST MOMENTS:

MORNING INTENTIONS

What's on my mind today?

_____

_____

_____

What deserves my energy and focus today?

_____

_____

What would being good to myself look like today?

_____

Ways I intend to feel grounded today:

○ THREE DEEP BREATHS

○ 60-SECOND BODY SCAN

○ MINDFUL CHECK-IN

I have the power to change:

_____

_____

_____

MY WORD OF THE DAY IS: _____

EVENING REFLECTIONS

What one thing can I be grateful for in this moment?

_____

I'm willing to let go of:

_____

Use this space to track how you practiced mindfulness throughout the day.

	WHEN	WHERE
MORNING		
AFTERNOON		
EVENING		

TODAY'S BEST MOMENTS:

MORNING INTENTIONS

What's on my mind today?

_____

_____

_____

What deserves my energy and focus today?

_____

_____

What would being good to myself look like today?

_____

Ways I intend to feel grounded today:

○ THREE DEEP BREATHS

○ 60-SECOND BODY SCAN

○ MINDFUL CHECK-IN

I have the power to change:

_____

_____

_____

MY WORD OF THE DAY IS: _____

EVENING REFLECTIONS

What one thing can I be grateful for in this moment?

_____

I'm willing to let go of:

_____

Use this space to track how you practiced mindfulness throughout the day.

	WHEN	WHERE
MORNING		
AFTERNOON		
EVENING		

TODAY'S BEST MOMENTS:

MORNING INTENTIONS

What's on my mind today?

_____

_____

_____

What deserves my energy and focus today?

_____

_____

What would being good to myself look like today?

_____

Ways I intend to feel grounded today:

○ THREE DEEP BREATHS

○ 60-SECOND BODY SCAN

○ MINDFUL CHECK-IN

I have the power to change:

_____

_____

_____

MY WORD OF THE DAY IS: _____

EVENING REFLECTIONS

What one thing can I be grateful for in this moment?

_____

I'm willing to let go of:

_____

Use this space to track how you practiced mindfulness throughout the day.

	WHEN	WHERE
MORNING		
AFTERNOON		
EVENING		

TODAY'S BEST MOMENTS:

MORNING INTENTIONS

What's on my mind today?

_____

_____

_____

What deserves my energy and focus today?

_____

_____

What would being good to myself look like today?

_____

Ways I intend to feel grounded today:

○ THREE DEEP BREATHS

○ 60-SECOND BODY SCAN

○ MINDFUL CHECK-IN

I have the power to change:

_____

_____

_____

MY WORD OF THE DAY IS: _____

EVENING REFLECTIONS

What one thing can I be grateful for in this moment?

_____

I'm willing to let go of:

_____

Use this space to track how you practiced mindfulness throughout the day.

	WHEN	WHERE
MORNING		
AFTERNOON		
EVENING		

TODAY'S BEST MOMENTS:

What's on my mind today?

_____

_____

_____

What deserves my energy and focus today?

_____

_____

What would being good to myself look like today?

_____

Ways I intend to feel grounded today:

○ THREE DEEP BREATHS

○ 60-SECOND BODY SCAN

○ MINDFUL CHECK-IN

I have the power to change:

_____

_____

_____

MY WORD OF THE DAY IS: _____

EVENING REFLECTIONS

What one thing can I be grateful for in this moment?

_____

I'm willing to let go of:

_____

Use this space to track how you practiced mindfulness throughout the day.

	WHEN	WHERE
MORNING		
AFTERNOON		
EVENING		

TODAY'S BEST MOMENTS:

MORNING INTENTIONS

What's on my mind today?

_____

_____

_____

What deserves my energy and focus today?

_____

_____

What would being good to myself look like today?

_____

Ways I intend to feel grounded today:

○ THREE DEEP BREATHS

○ 60-SECOND BODY SCAN

○ MINDFUL CHECK-IN

I have the power to change:

_____

_____

_____

MY WORD OF THE DAY IS: _____

EVENING REFLECTIONS

What one thing can I be grateful for in this moment?

_____

I'm willing to let go of:

_____

Use this space to track how you practiced mindfulness throughout the day.

	WHEN	WHERE
MORNING		
AFTERNOON		
EVENING		

TODAY'S BEST MOMENTS:

What's on my mind today?

_____

_____

_____

What deserves my energy and focus today?

_____

_____

What would being good to myself look like today?

_____

Ways I intend to feel grounded today:

○ THREE DEEP BREATHS

○ 60-SECOND BODY SCAN

○ MINDFUL CHECK-IN

I have the power to change:

_____

_____

_____

MY WORD OF THE DAY IS: _____

EVENING REFLECTIONS

What one thing can I be grateful for in this moment?

_____

I'm willing to let go of:

_____

Use this space to track how you practiced mindfulness throughout the day.

	WHEN	WHERE
MORNING		
AFTERNOON		
EVENING		

TODAY'S BEST MOMENTS:

MORNING INTENTIONS

What's on my mind today?

_____

_____

_____

What deserves my energy and focus today?

_____

_____

What would being good to myself look like today?

_____

Ways I intend to feel grounded today:

○ THREE DEEP BREATHS

○ 60-SECOND BODY SCAN

○ MINDFUL CHECK-IN

I have the power to change:

_____

_____

_____

MY WORD OF THE DAY IS: _____

EVENING REFLECTIONS

What one thing can I be grateful for in this moment?

_____

I'm willing to let go of:

_____

Use this space to track how you practiced mindfulness throughout the day.

	WHEN	WHERE
MORNING		
AFTERNOON		
EVENING		

TODAY'S BEST MOMENTS:

MORNING INTENTIONS

What's on my mind today?

_____

_____

_____

What deserves my energy and focus today?

_____

_____

What would being good to myself look like today?

_____

Ways I intend to feel grounded today:

◯ THREE DEEP BREATHS

◯ 60-SECOND BODY SCAN

◯ MINDFUL CHECK-IN

I have the power to change:

_____

_____

_____

MY WORD OF THE DAY IS: _____

EVENING REFLECTIONS

What one thing can I be grateful for in this moment?

_____

I'm willing to let go of:

_____

Use this space to track how you practiced mindfulness throughout the day.

	WHEN	WHERE
MORNING		
AFTERNOON		
EVENING		

TODAY'S BEST MOMENTS:

MORNING INTENTIONS

What's on my mind today?

_____

_____

_____

What deserves my energy and focus today?

_____

_____

What would being good to myself look like today?

_____

Ways I intend to feel grounded today:

○ THREE DEEP BREATHS

○ 60-SECOND BODY SCAN

○ MINDFUL CHECK-IN

I have the power to change:

_____

_____

_____

MY WORD OF THE DAY IS: _____

EVENING REFLECTIONS

What one thing can I be grateful for in this moment?

_____

I'm willing to let go of:

_____

Use this space to track how you practiced mindfulness throughout the day.

	WHEN	WHERE
MORNING		
AFTERNOON		
EVENING		

TODAY'S BEST MOMENTS:

What's on my mind today?

_____

_____

_____

What deserves my energy and focus today?

_____

_____

What would being good to myself look like today?

_____

Ways I intend to feel grounded today:

○ THREE DEEP BREATHS

○ 60-SECOND BODY SCAN

○ MINDFUL CHECK-IN

I have the power to change:

_____

_____

_____

MY WORD OF THE DAY IS: _____

EVENING REFLECTIONS

What one thing can I be grateful for in this moment?

_____

I'm willing to let go of:

_____

Use this space to track how you practiced mindfulness throughout the day.

	WHEN	WHERE
MORNING		
AFTERNOON		
EVENING		

TODAY'S BEST MOMENTS:

MORNING INTENTIONS

What's on my mind today?

_____

_____

_____

What deserves my energy and focus today?

_____

_____

What would being good to myself look like today?

_____

Ways I intend to feel grounded today:

○ THREE DEEP BREATHS

○ 60-SECOND BODY SCAN

○ MINDFUL CHECK-IN

I have the power to change:

_____

_____

_____

MY WORD OF THE DAY IS: _____

EVENING REFLECTIONS

What one thing can I be grateful for in this moment?

_____

I'm willing to let go of:

_____

Use this space to track how you practiced mindfulness throughout the day.

	WHEN	WHERE
MORNING		
AFTERNOON		
EVENING		

TODAY'S BEST MOMENTS:

DATE: ___ / ___ / ___

What's on my mind today?

_____

_____

_____

What deserves my energy and focus today?

_____

_____

What would being good to myself look like today?

_____

Ways I intend to feel grounded today:

○ THREE DEEP BREATHS

○ 60-SECOND BODY SCAN

○ MINDFUL CHECK-IN

I have the power to change:

_____

_____

_____

MY WORD OF THE DAY IS: _____

EVENING REFLECTIONS

What one thing can I be grateful for in this moment?

_____

I'm willing to let go of:

_____

Use this space to track how you practiced mindfulness throughout the day.

	WHEN	WHERE
MORNING		
AFTERNOON		
EVENING		

TODAY'S BEST MOMENTS:

DATE: ___ / ___ / ___

What's on my mind today?

_____

_____

_____

What deserves my energy and focus today?

_____

_____

What would being good to myself look like today?

_____

Ways I intend to feel grounded today:

○ THREE DEEP BREATHS

○ 60-SECOND BODY SCAN

○ MINDFUL CHECK-IN

I have the power to change:

_____

_____

_____

MY WORD OF THE DAY IS: _____

EVENING REFLECTIONS

What one thing can I be grateful for in this moment?

_____

I'm willing to let go of:

_____

Use this space to track how you practiced mindfulness throughout the day.

	WHEN	WHERE
MORNING		
AFTERNOON		
EVENING		

TODAY'S BEST MOMENTS:

MORNING INTENTIONS

What's on my mind today?

_____

_____

_____

What deserves my energy and focus today?

_____

_____

What would being good to myself look like today?

_____

Ways I intend to feel grounded today:

○ THREE DEEP BREATHS

○ 60-SECOND BODY SCAN

○ MINDFUL CHECK-IN

I have the power to change:

_____

_____

_____

MY WORD OF THE DAY IS: _____

EVENING REFLECTIONS

What one thing can I be grateful for in this moment?

I'm willing to let go of:

Use this space to track how you practiced mindfulness throughout the day.

	WHEN	WHERE
MORNING		
AFTERNOON		
EVENING		

TODAY'S BEST MOMENTS:

MORNING INTENTIONS

DATE: ___ / ___ / ___

What's on my mind today?

_____

_____

_____

What deserves my energy and focus today?

_____

_____

What would being good to myself look like today?

_____

Ways I intend to feel grounded today:

○ THREE DEEP BREATHS

○ 60-SECOND BODY SCAN

○ MINDFUL CHECK-IN

I have the power to change:

_____

_____

_____

MY WORD OF THE DAY IS: _____

EVENING REFLECTIONS

What one thing can I be grateful for in this moment?

_____

I'm willing to let go of:

_____

Use this space to track how you practiced mindfulness throughout the day.

	WHEN	WHERE
MORNING		
AFTERNOON		
EVENING		

TODAY'S BEST MOMENTS:

MORNING INTENTIONS

What's on my mind today?

_____

_____

_____

What deserves my energy and focus today?

_____

_____

What would being good to myself look like today?

_____

Ways I intend to feel grounded today:

○ THREE DEEP BREATHS

○ 60-SECOND BODY SCAN

○ MINDFUL CHECK-IN

I have the power to change:

_____

_____

_____

MY WORD OF THE DAY IS: _____

EVENING REFLECTIONS

What one thing can I be grateful for in this moment?

_____

I'm willing to let go of:

_____

Use this space to track how you practiced mindfulness throughout the day.

	WHEN	WHERE
MORNING		
AFTERNOON		
EVENING		

TODAY'S BEST MOMENTS:

MORNING INTENTIONS

What's on my mind today?

_____

_____

_____

What deserves my energy and focus today?

_____

_____

What would being good to myself look like today?

_____

Ways I intend to feel grounded today:

○ THREE DEEP BREATHS

○ 60-SECOND BODY SCAN

○ MINDFUL CHECK-IN

I have the power to change:

_____

_____

_____

MY WORD OF THE DAY IS: _____

EVENING REFLECTIONS

What one thing can I be grateful for in this moment?

_____

I'm willing to let go of:

_____

Use this space to track how you practiced mindfulness throughout the day.

	WHEN	WHERE
MORNING		
AFTERNOON		
EVENING		

TODAY'S BEST MOMENTS:

MORNING INTENTIONS

DATE: ___ / ___ / ___

What's on my mind today?

_____

_____

_____

What deserves my energy and focus today?

_____

_____

What would being good to myself look like today?

_____

Ways I intend to feel grounded today:

○ THREE DEEP BREATHS

○ 60-SECOND BODY SCAN

○ MINDFUL CHECK-IN

I have the power to change:

_____

_____

_____

MY WORD OF THE DAY IS: _____

EVENING REFLECTIONS

What one thing can I be grateful for in this moment?

_____

I'm willing to let go of:

_____

Use this space to track how you practiced mindfulness throughout the day.

	WHEN	WHERE
MORNING		
AFTERNOON		
EVENING		

TODAY'S BEST MOMENTS:

MORNING INTENTIONS

What's on my mind today?

_____

_____

_____

What deserves my energy and focus today?

_____

_____

What would being good to myself look like today?

_____

Ways I intend to feel grounded today:

○ THREE DEEP BREATHS

○ 60-SECOND BODY SCAN

○ MINDFUL CHECK-IN

I have the power to change:

_____

_____

_____

MY WORD OF THE DAY IS: _____

EVENING REFLECTIONS

What one thing can I be grateful for in this moment?

_____

I'm willing to let go of:

_____

Use this space to track how you practiced mindfulness throughout the day.

	WHEN	WHERE
MORNING		
AFTERNOON		
EVENING		

TODAY'S BEST MOMENTS:

MORNING INTENTIONS

DATE: ___ / ___ / ___

What's on my mind today?

_____

_____

_____

What deserves my energy and focus today?

_____

_____

What would being good to myself look like today?

_____

Ways I intend to feel grounded today:

○ THREE DEEP BREATHS

○ 60-SECOND BODY SCAN

○ MINDFUL CHECK-IN

I have the power to change:

_____

_____

_____

MY WORD OF THE DAY IS: _____

EVENING REFLECTIONS

What one thing can I be grateful for in this moment?

_____

I'm willing to let go of:

_____

Use this space to track how you practiced mindfulness throughout the day.

	WHEN	WHERE
MORNING		
AFTERNOON		
EVENING		

TODAY'S BEST MOMENTS:

MORNING INTENTIONS

What's on my mind today?

_____

_____

_____

What deserves my energy and focus today?

_____

_____

What would being good to myself look like today?

_____

Ways I intend to feel grounded today:

○ THREE DEEP BREATHS

○ 60-SECOND BODY SCAN

○ MINDFUL CHECK-IN

I have the power to change:

_____

_____

_____

MY WORD OF THE DAY IS: _____

EVENING REFLECTIONS

What one thing can I be grateful for in this moment?

_____

I'm willing to let go of:

_____

Use this space to track how you practiced mindfulness throughout the day.

	WHEN	WHERE
MORNING		
AFTERNOON		
EVENING		

TODAY'S BEST MOMENTS:

MORNING INTENTIONS

What's on my mind today?

_____

_____

_____

What deserves my energy and focus today?

_____

_____

What would being good to myself look like today?

_____

Ways I intend to feel grounded today:

○ THREE DEEP BREATHS

○ 60-SECOND BODY SCAN

○ MINDFUL CHECK-IN

I have the power to change:

_____

_____

_____

MY WORD OF THE DAY IS: _____

EVENING REFLECTIONS

What one thing can I be grateful for in this moment?

_____

I'm willing to let go of:

_____

Use this space to track how you practiced mindfulness throughout the day.

	WHEN	WHERE
MORNING		
AFTERNOON		
EVENING		

TODAY'S BEST MOMENTS:

MORNING INTENTIONS

What's on my mind today?

_____

_____

_____

What deserves my energy and focus today?

_____

_____

What would being good to myself look like today?

_____

Ways I intend to feel grounded today:

○ THREE DEEP BREATHS

○ 60-SECOND BODY SCAN

○ MINDFUL CHECK-IN

I have the power to change:

_____

_____

_____

MY WORD OF THE DAY IS: _____

EVENING REFLECTIONS

What one thing can I be grateful for in this moment?

_____

I'm willing to let go of:

_____

Use this space to track how you practiced mindfulness throughout the day.

	WHEN	WHERE
MORNING		
AFTERNOON		
EVENING		

TODAY'S BEST MOMENTS:

MORNING INTENTIONS

What's on my mind today?

_____

_____

_____

What deserves my energy and focus today?

_____

_____

What would being good to myself look like today?

_____

Ways I intend to feel grounded today:

○ THREE DEEP BREATHS

○ 60-SECOND BODY SCAN

○ MINDFUL CHECK-IN

I have the power to change:

_____

_____

_____

MY WORD OF THE DAY IS: _____

EVENING REFLECTIONS

What one thing can I be grateful for in this moment?

_____

I'm willing to let go of:

_____

Use this space to track how you practiced mindfulness throughout the day.

	WHEN	WHERE
MORNING		
AFTERNOON		
EVENING		

TODAY'S BEST MOMENTS:

MORNING INTENTIONS

What's on my mind today?

_____

_____

_____

What deserves my energy and focus today?

_____

_____

What would being good to myself look like today?

_____

Ways I intend to feel grounded today:

○ THREE DEEP BREATHS

○ 60-SECOND BODY SCAN

○ MINDFUL CHECK-IN

I have the power to change:

_____

_____

_____

MY WORD OF THE DAY IS: _____

EVENING REFLECTIONS

What one thing can I be grateful for in this moment?

_____

I'm willing to let go of:

_____

Use this space to track how you practiced mindfulness throughout the day.

	WHEN	WHERE
MORNING		
AFTERNOON		
EVENING		

TODAY'S BEST MOMENTS:

MORNING INTENTIONS

DATE: ___ / ___ / ___

What's on my mind today?

_____

_____

_____

What deserves my energy and focus today?

_____

_____

What would being good to myself look like today?

_____

Ways I intend to feel grounded today:

○ THREE DEEP BREATHS

○ 60-SECOND BODY SCAN

○ MINDFUL CHECK-IN

I have the power to change:

_____

_____

_____

MY WORD OF THE DAY IS: _____

EVENING REFLECTIONS

What one thing can I be grateful for in this moment?

_____

I'm willing to let go of:

_____

Use this space to track how you practiced mindfulness throughout the day.

	WHEN	WHERE
MORNING		
AFTERNOON		
EVENING		

TODAY'S BEST MOMENTS:

DATE: ___ / ___ / ___

What's on my mind today?

_____

_____

_____

What deserves my energy and focus today?

_____

_____

What would being good to myself look like today?

_____

Ways I intend to feel grounded today:

○ THREE DEEP BREATHS

○ 60-SECOND BODY SCAN

○ MINDFUL CHECK-IN

I have the power to change:

_____

_____

_____

MY WORD OF THE DAY IS: _____

EVENING REFLECTIONS

What one thing can I be grateful for in this moment?

_____

I'm willing to let go of:

_____

Use this space to track how you practiced mindfulness throughout the day.

	WHEN	WHERE
MORNING		
AFTERNOON		
EVENING		

TODAY'S BEST MOMENTS:

MORNING INTENTIONS

What's on my mind today?

_____

_____

_____

What deserves my energy and focus today?

_____

_____

What would being good to myself look like today?

_____

Ways I intend to feel grounded today:

○ THREE DEEP BREATHS

○ 60-SECOND BODY SCAN

○ MINDFUL CHECK-IN

I have the power to change:

_____

_____

_____

MY WORD OF THE DAY IS: _____

EVENING REFLECTIONS

What one thing can I be grateful for in this moment?

_____

I'm willing to let go of:

_____

Use this space to track how you practiced mindfulness throughout the day.

	WHEN	WHERE
MORNING		
AFTERNOON		
EVENING		

TODAY'S BEST MOMENTS:

MORNING INTENTIONS

What's on my mind today?

_____

_____

_____

What deserves my energy and focus today?

_____

_____

What would being good to myself look like today?

_____

Ways I intend to feel grounded today:

○ THREE DEEP BREATHS

○ 60-SECOND BODY SCAN

○ MINDFUL CHECK-IN

I have the power to change:

_____

_____

_____

MY WORD OF THE DAY IS: _____

EVENING REFLECTIONS

What one thing can I be grateful for in this moment?

_____

I'm willing to let go of:

_____

Use this space to track how you practiced mindfulness throughout the day.

	WHEN	WHERE
MORNING		
AFTERNOON		
EVENING		

TODAY'S BEST MOMENTS:

ABOUT THE AUTHOR

 **KRISTEN MANIERI** is a Certified Habits Coach, as well as a Certified Mindfulness Teacher through the International Mindfulness Teachers Association (IMTA). The author of *Better Daily Mindfulness Habits*, Kristen believes that when we actively engage in our growth and evolution, we can begin to live a more conscious, connected, and intentional life. Besides being a writer and coach, Kristen is the host of the *60 Mindful Minutes* podcast, which launched in 2017 and has produced inspiring and thought-provoking interviews with over 130 authors. Kristen holds a BA in English literature and communication studies. She shares her life with her two daughters, her husband, and their three cats. Connect with her at KristenManieri.com or on Instagram @kristenmanieri_.